Divorce Mediation from the Inside Out

A Mindful Approach to Divorce

Ora Schwartzberg, Esq.

Divorce Mediation from the Inside Out:
A Mindful Approach to Divorce

Published by Wheatmark®
610 East Delano Street, Suite 104
Tucson, Arizona 85705 U.S.A.
www.wheatmark.com

ISBN: 978-1-60494-175-3
LCCN: 2008934796

Preface

This book is addressed to people who are considering the various options available for getting a divorce. Its purpose is to inform the *general public* about the benefits of obtaining a mediated divorce.

This book is *not* written for lawyers or for mediators and does not attempt to describe any specific methodology or provide instruction for conducting effective mediations. That topic is reserved for a later book.

The author does provide training in mediation for attorneys and mediators, as well as for business organizations. Information regarding such training is available at her website, www.nhlawyer.net.

Dedication

This book is dedicated to Gertrude, Harold, and Richard, the three people who always believed in me and taught me that I was capable of accomplishing anything I chose to pursue; and to my children, Jesse, Ezra, and Eli, the three people to whom I try to impart this same gift.

Contents

Head Prep

The outcome of your divorce mediation depends, in large part, whether you approach it from the inside out.

During my twenty-three years of practice as a divorce attorney/mediator, I have learned from my clients that maintaining integrity is the only thing that really matters. Having integrity means doing the right thing. It isn't about getting the most money or the most scheduled time with the kids. It is about self-examination and a willingness to act consistently with one's beliefs, regardless of how difficult it may be to take such action. It is about developing resolutions that are consistent with our character and our concepts of the person that we want to continue to become.

Doing the right thing does not mean giving in to the demands of the other spouse; it means paying attention to our emotions, noticing our body's internal reactions, and then acting consistently with this information.

We all want to have a rewarding and successful life in which we appreciate our ability to make choices and learn from some of the bad choices we may have made in the past. Mediation offers this opportunity. Many of my clients have used this opportunity to lay the groundwork for developing a better way of being that will continue to serve them well in the next phase of their lives.

These are the people with courage, a necessary component of integrity. My clients who have courage are not fearless, but they are not afraid to notice and pay careful attention to their experience of being fearful. These clients understand that courage means looking fear in the face (such as fear of loneliness, poverty, or self-loathing), recognizing that it exists, and allowing such fear to transform into positive energy.

I also work with many clients who lack courage. These are the victims of divorce who are also usually life's victims. Their failure to approach a difficult situation with courage results in them letting things happen and then being angry about the outcome. This, too, often changes during the mediation process, and when it does, such clients begin to develop the courage to create a life that was never before accessible.

The only thing that really matters is integrity, but there cannot be integrity without self-knowledge. Through the mediation process, couples learn to be more mindful of their emotions and their body's internal reactions and are thus better able to access knowledge about what is truly important to each of them. It is by using this knowledge and understanding the process of how to continue to access self-knowledge that mediation can facilitate the development of a personal blueprint for how people conduct their future endeavors ...

... if they choose to do it mindfully from the inside out.

The Cost of It!

Divorce is expensive, and the resulting aftermath can devastate a family for a long period of time. Mediation minimizes this expense and the continuing aftershocks of the initial destruction.

Some of the costs associated with divorce are:

- Attorney's fees/mediator fees

- Time lost from work/job loss/lost opportunity

- Stress/illness/psychological trauma

- Trauma for children

ATTORNEY'S FEES/MEDIATOR FEES

Divorces in which the financial issues or child  living arrangements are in dispute commonly cost in excess of twenty-five thousand dollars per spouse. Cases involving complicated property division or support issues may exceed fifty thousand dollars per spouse. These cases can take as long as two to three years to get through the courts.

In contrast, these same kinds of cases often have a total combined cost for both spouses of less than ten thousand dollars in mediation and attorney fees when divorcing couples choose to go to mediation prior to bringing a court action. The time required to finalize a mediated divorce is often less than six months.

Mediated divorces usually cost less even though the hourly rate for mediators is often similar to the hourly rate charged by attorneys. The cost is less because the time required by the mediator and the attorneys in a mediated divorce is substantially less than the time required of two separate attorneys to proceed with a divorce through the court system.

This is due in part to the fact that a lot of time and money for attorney's fees are used, during the initial stages of the divorce proceedings, to litigate peripheral issues, for the purpose of posturing and intimidation. Clients often find themselves going to court numerous times to litigate various issues that have very little significance to the final outcome of their case.

For example, one spouse may seek court intervention to order the other spouse to pay certain expenses, on a temporary basis, or for a determination as to who has the right to reside in the home during the divorce proceedings. These are often two hotly contested issues in which each of the opposing attorneys seeks to gain a psychological advantage over the other by "winning" a favorable decision early in the litigation.

Also, issues involving the failure of one side to produce necessary documents, or answer certain questions, can tie up a divorce case for two or three years. This rarely occurs during the mediation process because the agreement to mediate includes an agreement to provide all documents and information requested by the mediator. Refusal to do so will terminate the mediation.

Unfortunately, one of the most widely used tactics for litigating such temporary or peripheral issues is the character assassination of the opposing spouse during court appearances. Once this begins, clients are willing to continue to fund their attorneys to protect them from what they perceive to be a potentially devastating outcome.

Another factor that leads to protracted/expensive divorce litigation is the conflict of interests between the client and attorney. Most attorneys require substantial retainers (between five and ten thousand dollars) before they begin a case, as well as replenishment retainers, as the case proceeds. The attorney then charges an hourly rate which is credited against the retainer. If the attorney settles the case, the attorney is required to return any unused portion of the retainer to the client. The more time it takes to resolve any divorce case, the more money the attorney makes.

Mediators generally operate under a different kind of financial structure. They make money by working with a greater number of clients for shorter periods of time. A good mediator develops a reputation for helping their clients to reach a resolution of their divorce issues quickly. Some mediators will further limit the clients' financial exposure and fear of escalating costs by charging a set fee for preparing all of the paperwork once the clients have reached an agreement.

Once the paperwork has been completed, mediation clients are encouraged to take the divorce documents to separate "consulting" attorneys for review. These documents should include the divorce agreement as well as all financial backup materials such as recent retirement account and bank statements, appraisals, mortgage balance statements, and tax returns.

The consulting attorney will generally charge for only a couple of hours (not a substantial retainer) to review the divorce documents.

The net result is less time spent by all and less money spent by the client.

TIME LOSS FROM WORK/ JOB LOSS/LOST OPPORTUNITY

The time commitment required to prepare for and attend court proceedings depletes available time, energy, and resources  that could be used to enhance each spouse's job performance or pursuit of financial opportunities.

The stress of a litigated divorce can be so debilitating that litigating spouses are often not able to perform their jobs at even a minimal level of competence. As a result, it is not uncommon for people who are going through divorces to lose their jobs or experience business failures.

Mediation conserves time, emotional energy, and financial resources, and it enables spouses to move forward without having to recover from the destructive side effects experienced during the court proceedings.

STRESS/ILLNESS/ PSYCHOLOGICAL TRAUMA

It is also not unusual for a person to become seriously ill while going through a divorce. The fear of the unknown, the psychological trauma that results from experiencing the behavior of the other spouse (both inside and outside of the courtroom), and the need to deal with issues of parent-child relationships can be overwhelming.

Mediation brings the issues of finances and child rearing out into the open, to be addressed and resolved through coopera-tion. Even though each spouse may not get the exact result that they think they want, they do get a resolution, and with that reso-lution comes the opportunity to go forward and rebuild.

Nothing can be more difficult than encountering the unknown and experiencing the feeling of impo-tence associated with being unable to navigate to the other side. Mediation provides the tools to get through a divorce without leaving a wake of devastation.

TRAUMA FOR CHILDREN

One of the strongest reasons to mediate is to pro-tect your children. It is difficult enough for children to adjust to the reality that the family that they trusted would continue to exist is breaking apart. Children look to their parents for guidance and to help them make sense of what is going on in their home.

Children who experience parents who treat each other with respect and who are also able to remain available to their children and other responsibilities, even during a divorce, are more likely to model such behavior and to perceive the world in a more positive light.

Mediation allows couples to maintain their integrity and to continue to present themselves to their children as the kind of parents they would be proud to see their children become.

Why the Courts Can't Effectively Resolve Divorce Issues

The courts are good at resolving financial issues between strangers and associates. It is only by default that the courts have taken the job of resolving financial and parenting issues associated with the breakup of a family.

The courts are ill-equipped to resolve family issues because of the complex psychological, cultural, and societal issues that must be balanced in order to reach a fair and empowering resolution for parents and children.

No matter how well-intentioned a judge may be,

the court system does not provide a forum conducive to resolving family disputes. Even our best trial attorneys often cannot achieve a good resolution for their clients without the devastating collateral financial and emotional damage to both parents and children.

Attorneys are train-ed to do whatever is necessary to get the best possible result for their clients. The "best possible result" in litigation between strangers and associates is defined as "the most money and/ or the most power and control." A goal such as this, even if achieved, does  not necessarily translate to a good result for any family member in a divorce, including the one who "wins."

A good resolution of the kinds of issues involved with the breakup of a marriage is one that allocates money and control so that both husband and wife have a reasonable opportunity to move forward in a positive direction with their lives. The goal of trying to "get more" or to "get the most" usually creates excessive legal expenses and far more animosity in families than is created by the family breakup itself.

Many of our court systems, including the New Hampshire courts where I practice, have recognized the inability of the courts to adequately resolve family disputes, especially because of the high demand family issues put on the courts' time. The courts are beginning to recognize how mediation, working in concert with our judiciary, enables the participants in the breakup of a marriage to develop their own resolutions.

Resolutions developed by the participants in a divorce case tend to be more fair and tend to more specifically address potential future problems than decisions developed by the courts. Furthermore, the methods by which husbands and wives develop these resolutions empower them to create positive outcomes while maintaining their integrity and respect for each other.

Paths to Finalizing a Divorce

There are three paths to finalizing a divorce:

Path One

- Spouses participate in mediation and reach

an agreement on all financial and parenting
issues
- Spouses submit a mediated agreement to
the court
- Court issues divorce decree, which includes
a mediated agreement

Path Two

- One spouse files for divorce and has the
other spouse served
- Spouses participate in a court hearing on
temporary issues (parenting issues, support, service of debt and use of property)
- Court issues an order on temporary matters
- Spouses participate in discovery process
(parties exchange financial documents and
relevant information)
- Spouses participate in a hearing to decide
all financial and parenting issues
- Court issues a divorce decree based on the
testimony and evidence provided by each
of the spouses at the contested hearing

Path Three

- Spouses reach a settlement (with or without a
mediator) any time along Path Two, and the
settlement agreement becomes part of the divorce decree.

WHY CHOOSE PATH ONE?

Path One is usually the quickest, least expensive path, and is also the path most likely to result in the most fair, most comprehensive divorce decree. Both spouses are generally more cooperative and open to creativity if they pursue Path One, because Path One encourages open communication. Such communication is quickly cut off in court proceedings that require each spouse to assume an adversarial posture.

Why Divorce Mediation Works

MINIMIZES THE FEAR OF THE UNKNOWN

Divorce mediation clients soon learn that there are wide varieties of financial and parenting resolutions that could be incorporated into their divorce decree. Mediation clients are encouraged to focus on many possible alternatives. This is quite different from the focus developed by the clients who choose to litigate their cases in the courts. Litigants tend to focus on developing the best possible resolution for themselves and to focus all of their attention and legal fees on getting exactly that. *It isn't until months or years into the litigation that they are forced to face the fact that the resolution that they formulated is not going to be the end result.*

During the mediation process, each spouse has an opportunity to examine the best and worst possible resolutions for each of them and at least initially to put some parameters around the unknown. Because they are in direct communication with each other throughout the process, they don't have to fear being unprepared to address previously unknown demands during court proceedings.

Through mediation, both spouses become keenly aware of the fact that they are in a much better position to create a resolution of their divorce issues than to allow a court to do it for them.

BUILDS ON COMMON AND UNIQUE INTERESTS AND GOALS

Divorcing spouses always have some common interests and goals. In particular they both want to get through the divorce process in a way that minimizes the financial and emotional pain. Most people want to do the right thing in dealing with their former partner and more often than not do not want to cause their soon-to-be ex-spouse unnecessary pain. They also almost always have concerns about minimizing any trauma to their children.

Divorcing spouses also always have some unique interests and goals that need to be communicated to the other, if such unique interests and goals are to be considered in crafting a resolution.

Mediation brings couples together with a trained

professional who teaches them how to communicate and how to develop such goals. A good mediator will show them how to notice their emotions and their bodies' reactions to the various options being explored during the mediation process. The mediator will then assist them in using this information to clarify and further explore what should be included in any resolution or settlement. It is through this kind mutual mindful communication that good resolutions evolve.

ELICITS CREATIVITY AND UNIQUE RESOLUTIONS

It is usually when each spouse gets in touch with their own interests and goals, and with those of the other, that they are able to use their joint creativity to develop unique resolutions.

Through the mediation process, couples learn to reframe the divorce process from being a way of dealing with a terrible loss to an opportunity for personal growth and evolution. Once this bridge is crossed, creative solutions quickly surface.

What Can Go Wrong?

If you have a competent mediator, the success of mediation depends on the attitude of the participants. I have never had a failed mediation in which all parties acted in good faith. Some of the behaviors associated with failed mediations are as follows:

- Stonewalling
- Blaming and punishing
- Bullying
- Hiding assets and information
- Attorney interference

STONEWALLING

Just like the mason who tears down his work and starts over and over again because one stone doesn't fit just right, the stone-walling spouse appears to be working diligently to reach various agreements, only to change his or her mind once it appears that the major issues in dispute have been resolved.

This behavior is often exhibited by a spouse who does not want a divorce and who uses this behavior (sometimes unconsciously) to forestall the inevitable. Unless the mediator recognizes and effectively deals with this, the couple will perceive that they are at an impasse and will leave the mediation in frustration, only to turn the job of resolving their divorce issues over to the court.

Sometimes stonewalling may be an indicator that a decision to divorce has been made prematurely, and one or both spouses are crying out to give the marriage another chance. I have seen several such stonewalling cases resulting in an agreement to seek marriage counseling or to take steps to resolve the conflicts within the marriage. Although mediation usually terminates quickly in such cases, these cases are among the successful mediations that have brought couples to an unexpected resolution.

Blaming and Punishing

Some people attempt to use mediation as a forum in which to blame the other spouse for the failure of the marriage. With this goal in mind, they often try to form an alliance with the mediator  to punish their "bad" spouse for transgressions that occurred during the marriage.

Although it is sometimes helpful for an angry spouse to express his or her feelings associated with certain perceived wrongdoings of the other, it is the job of the mediator to direct the couple's attention toward the issues that must be resolved in order to legally end their marriage.

Sometimes a brief divergence into the circumstances surrounding some of the difficulties that led to the demise of the marriage can make it easier for a couple to work through the mediation process, especially if it leads to the expression of positive feelings or even an apology, but this requires tremendous skill and sensitivity on the part of the mediator.

It is the role of the mediator not to allow negative feelings to interfere with the couple's perception of how to fairly resolve their divorce issues. A competent mediator understands that failed marriages are usually the result of the actions of both parties and will divert attempts to use guilt or blame as the basis for resolving financial or childrearing issues.

When one or both parties cannot get beyond the need to punish the other for their failed marriage, the punishing party will often seek court assistance to carry out their punishments. It may take years for the punishing spouse to learn that courts generally aren't very effective forums for carrying out such punishments.

Attempts to punish should not be confused with discussions about bad behavior on the part of either spouse for the purpose of creating a fair agreement. Sometimes the acts of either or both spouses have financial or parenting ramifications that should not be ignored during the mediation process. The relevance of behavioral issues is discussed in detail in the chapter "How to Decide What's Fair."

BULLYING

In marriages with a long history of power imbalance—where one person makes the decisions and the other goes along with them—the decision-making spouse may perceive mediation as a means of continuing to get what he or she wants,

irrespective of legal rights or objective concepts of fairness.

These couples will often enter the mediation after having reached an agreement on all of the issues. Such an agreement will usually be extremely favorable to the more powerful spouse, but both spouses will assure the mediator that this is what they both want, and therefore this agreement should be adopted by the court.

As the mediation progresses, it often becomes apparent that the less powerful spouse knows that the proposed agreement is unfair, but will do anything to avoid conflict with the other spouse. This is especially likely when the weaker spouse does not have available financial resources to take the case to court.

The more powerful spouse knows from experience that if he or she just keeps at the other, the weaker spouse will agree to an extremely unfair divorce settlement.

In some jurisdictions, the courts will step in and refuse to approve such agreements, especially with respect to its effect on children, but some courts will approve just about anything.

In such cases, the only possibility of reaching anything close to a fair resolution is through the courts. Unfortunately, the less powerful spouse rarely perceives court action, or even the threat of it, as a viable option.

HIDING ASSETS AND INFORMATION

Sometimes a person will choose mediation over

litigation because they believe
that they can get their spouse to
agree to settle without becoming
aware of certain assets or information.

Such an individual also often
perceives the mediator as some-
one who can be duped, pushed
around, or otherwise controlled
so that hidden documentation
never has to be disclosed.

Full disclosure of information is a mandatory part
of the mediation process, and any failure or refusal
to disclose documentation or information should im-
mediately end it. Full cooperation and disclosure is
a basic ground rule of mediation, and without it, no
mediation can go forward in good faith.

A competent mediator will end the mediation if this
becomes an issue. The parties will then have the option
of going to court and having the court rule on whether
or not certain documentation has to be provided.

Once this issue has been resolved by the courts,
mediation is again possible.

ATTORNEY INTERFERENCE

Divorcing couples are usually more cooperative
in working to resolve their conflicts than are their attorneys. Attorneys are trained to be positional and to
simplify the issues into clear wins and losses for their
clients. They are trained to avoid any losses and to
fight to the bitter end to get the most for their clients.

Divorcing couples usually understand that they can't have everything their way, and that negotiating in good faith brings other rewards like a quicker resolution of their divorce and less emotional and financial damage to themselves and their children.

Their attorneys don't always have similar motivations. From the attorneys' perspective, the longer the divorce takes, the more money they make, and the greater opportunity they have to show off their skills as a litigator.

It is not that unusual for a client to want to settle a case in mediation, but upon advice of counsel withdraw from the mediation and turn to the court to decide the outstanding issues. Rather than give up on the mediation, some couples are able to get beyond such an impasse by consulting with different attorneys about the issues in dispute and the progress of the mediation.

MEDIATION RESCUE

There should be a sense of progress as a couple proceeds with mediation. If either or both parties feel like they are getting nowhere after three or more sessions, or if they remain stuck on one particular issue, this should be discussed with the mediator. If such a discussion does not satisfy either party that progress is being made, it usually means that it is time to leave the mediation.

It is not unusual to be successful with a second mediator even though very little or nothing was accomplished with the first mediator. This is because there are enormous differences from mediator to mediator with respect to quality of service and competence.

How to Decide What's Fair—When Behavior Counts!

The only people with enough information to make a determination of fairness are the two people getting divorced. Much of this information can remain inaccessible, however, due to the fact that it has to be filtered through the perceptions and emotions of two individuals with potentially conflicting interests. A good mediator knows how to extract this information to help the couple decide what is relevant and what is not.

Clearly, any financial information is relevant to decisions regarding the distribution of property and support. This is generally made readily available during the mediation process.

More difficult to uncover and interpret are the actions and acts of omission by each of the parties during the marriage. Some are relevant to the financial settlement and childrearing arrangements, and some are not.

It is not enough for one party to demonstrate that there was bad behavior on the part of the other spouse. What is crucial is that, if bad behavior did occur, it had a negative financial impact on the other spouse, or it provides a reliable indicator of limitations on that spouse's ability to effectively parent. In such cases, it is important to examine the impact of this behavior on the current financial and parenting situation.

Without a strong nexus between a particular behavior and the present financial or childrearing realities, information about bad behavior is not especially helpful.

In order to illustrate what may form a nexus between bad behavior, the distribution of the marital estate, and the determination of parental responsibilities, I will describe a few hypothetical cases.

VICKIE THE VULNERABLE AND SAM THE SAVIOR

Vickie met her husband, Sam, while in rehab for drug addiction. She was in a residential facility for two months and Sam was her counselor. After a successful rehab, Vickie returned home and resumed management of her extremely lucrative beauty salon and spa.

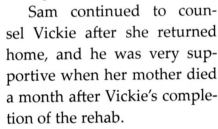

Sam continued to counsel Vickie after she returned home, and he was very supportive when her mother died a month after Vickie's completion of the rehab.

Soon after Vickie's mother's death, Sam convinced Vickie that they were soul mates, destined to spend their lives together. Vickie sold her salon and spa and moved several hundred miles away to be with Sam. Vickie used some of the proceeds from the sale of the salon and spa to pay Sam's debts. She also bought them both vehicles. They used the rest of the money to take vacations together.

The couple married two months later and Vickie became pregnant. She had a miscarriage. Four other miscarriages shortly followed. Vickie took a job at the rehab center, working for a fraction of what she had been earning in her own business Sam continued to work at the rehab center and earned $150,000 per year.

After two years of marriage, Sam announced that he wanted a divorce. Although he denied seeing anyone else, Vickie had observed his interactions with one of the recovering residents at the rehab center and felt very uncomfortable about the obvious affection they expressed toward each other.

Vickie has a high school education and no ability to get a job that pays more than $12 per hour. She does not have any money left to start a new business.

The Nexus

Vickie gave up her means of support because of Sam's promise that they could create a life together. After two years, his attention is elsewhere and she can no longer support herself in the manner to which she had become accustomed without his help.

Query

Should Sam have an obligation to support Vickie or provide her with a cash settlement because of the financial losses Vickie incurred?

GRANT THE AUTHOR AND PAULA THE PROVIDER

When Grant and Paula met, he was in the process of writing his first novel and expected to be able to bring in some extra money with royalties once the novel was published. For the past two years he had been working on the novel and living off an inheritance from his uncle, which was now almost depleted. He had no other assets or sources of income.

Paula is a physician with an income of $200,000 per year. The couple married six months after they met and have been married for two years. They agreed that she would support him until he finished his novel, and then he would seek employment.

Paula recently discovered that Grant had been spending a lot of time with other women, and she believes that he has been cheating on her for almost the entire marriage. She has told Grant that she wants a divorce. Grant is still writing his novel, has no other means of support, and is requesting that she continue to support him until he is able to obtain full-time employment.

The Nexus

Grant has no means of support because of his arrangement with Paula and her agreement to support him. Paula feels that he made this arrangement with her under false pretenses.

Query

Should Paula have to continue to support Grant and if so for how long?

MARJORIE THE MOM AND DAN THE DANGEROUS

Marjorie has been a stay-at-home mom for the past ten years; she is the primary caretaker of the parties' three children, ages ten, eight, and five. She has an advanced teaching decree and acknowledges that she can get a job teaching with a salary of $45,000 per year.

Dan was working more than full time as a financial analyst, earning $125,000 per year, when he lost his job two years ago after being wrongly accused of embezzling money from his employer. He is unemployable in that industry, but he was able to get a teaching job making $45,000 per year.

Six months ago Marjorie told Dan's current employer about the embezzlement allegations, and Dan was fired. He has not been able to obtain employment since then.

Marjorie has told the children that their father is a dangerous man, and she has done everything she can to limit their contact with him. In order to further create a case for Dan's bad behavior, she has made false reports to the police regarding seatbelt violations and has reported him for driving an unsafe vehicle. She has also reported him to the town for having an improperly insulated home and being in violation of various building codes and zoning regulations, which she believes creates an unsafe environment for the children.

Relevant Nexus

Marjorie's behavior is having a negative effect on the children's relationship with Dan and his ability to parent the children.

Query

Where should the children live, and who shall be given greater parental responsibility? How are the children to be supported?

Bad Behavior as a Topic for Discussion

These are obviously one-sided examples, used for the sake of illustration. The real cases from which they were taken had some counterbalancing behaviors on the other side. In each of these cases, discussion of spousal behavior would probably be helpful to the process of reaching an agreement.

It is sometimes important for mediation participants to have the opportunity to examine and attempt to understand marital behaviors. With this knowledge and understanding, a joint decision can be made as to what effect, if any, such behavior should have on the terms of the settlement agreement.

The Law of It

An effective mediator educates their clients about the applicable law of their state. This information provides a frame of reference for how the courts in a particular state determine fairness. It also puts the clients on notice that an agreement, which will be consistent with their personal perception of fairness, may differ greatly from some generic concept of fairness that is likely to be generated by the court.

Divorce law is quite different from state to state. This is a clear indication that there are many variables that contribute to the fairness of a divorce decree, and that there is more than one fair way to resolve any particular issue.

Some of the legal issues to discuss with a mediator are as follows:

- Does the law provide for a fifty/fifty division of assets or may one of us be entitled to more? If so how is that determined?

- How are various assets valued when calculating the division of assets:
  - The home
  - Other real estate
  - IRAs, 401Ks, and other retirement assets
  - Pensions
  - Business investments
  - Stock options

- How is the debt associated with a particular asset divided?

- Who is responsible for the credit cards?

- How is the house or its value distributed? Who may live in the house and under what conditions? Does it matter whose name is on the title?

- How are family gifts or inheritances to one spouse handled?

- Does the law require the division of premarital assets or debts?

- How is a business divided? Is there any consideration given to the contributions of each spouse to the value?

- How are stock options divided?

- How are pensions that will provide a stream of income in the future distributed?

- Who may receive what tax deductions?

- What are the ramifications of requiring life insurance?

- Does the law provide for spousal support, and if so, under what conditions?

- Does the reason for the divorce have any bearing on the distribution of property or parental rights?

- Can the children live with both parents? What are some options?

- How is child support determined? Does the parenting schedule have an impact on the amount of child support?

- What is the law with respect to one parent relocating with the children?

- What are the tax ramifications associated with

the distribution of property, spousal support, child support, and parenting arrangements?

It is likely that the mediator will not be able to provide definitive answers to all of these questions, either because of the ambiguity of the law or because of the mediator's lack of expertise in a particular area.

These questions should always be raised, however, and if a good mediator is not able to adequately address a particular issue, they will refer you to an appropriate professional, such as an attorney, tax advisor, financial planner, or appraiser.

What's Your Plan?

D ivorce can be an opportunity for individuals to take a fresh look at who they are and who they would like to become. Couples who approach mediation while simultaneously examining their own values, aspirations, and options are in a better position to develop a mediated divorce agreement that serves their future needs.

When couples are able to develop even rudimentary visions for their separate futures, they are better equipped to define the terms of the divorce agreement accordingly. It projects the settlement negotiations into new realms of possibilities. *Unlike the divorce attorney whose focus is reaching an agreement that translates into the most dollars for their client, couples with visions for their futures are able to consider various options for settlement that may not equate to a quantifiable dollar amount.*

Spouses with plans are usually less focused on dollars because their plans provide a more realistic perspective from which to assess the value of a partic-ular settlement agreement. Because of this perspective, they are usually able to recognize the fact that the difference between receiving the most amount of money possible or some lesser amount will have little or no effect on their future. It is the people who have no idea about what they want their future lives to look like who focus on the need for the most—"just in case ..."

Mediation sessions offer an excellent opportunity for couples to work with the mediator to begin to develop a sense of what is important for their respective futures. Once identified, such elements of importance can be integrated into their divorce agreement.

How to Choose a Mediator

Experience and passion are the two active ingredients for a good mediator. The best way to evaluate this is to speak directly with any mediator being considered. A lot can be learned by speaking with the mediator on the phone, asking key questions, and then listening attentively to the mediator's answers, tone of voice, and ability or inability to create an immediate rapport.

It is important that the mediator have substantial experience both with mediation and the practice of divorce law in your jurisdiction. The mediator does not have to be an attorney, but they should be extremely knowledgeable about how the divorce laws are being applied where you live.

It is also critical that the mediator know how to draft a tight, clear agreement that precisely reflects your intentions and does not create any unintended future problems. For example, a competent mediator will know what can go wrong if a couple continues to share ownership of their home or other substantial asset after the divorce, and how to draft an agreement to protect against such potential problems.

The most important question that you can ask a mediator, however, is not one about their skills but about *why* they are doing divorce mediation. A good mediator will always answer that question with passion. Their responses will convey a sense of purpose in their own lives about doing something that really matters. In most cases, they will strongly recommend the mediation process because of their genuine belief that a decision to mediate is likely to be a pivotal point for launching a more rewarding life.

It will be obvious that mediation is not just their job or a way to make money, but more importantly a projection of who the mediator is and how their values have been incorporated into this particular line of service.

How to Prepare for Your First Mediation Session

The appendix contains a set of forms that when completed will, in most cases, provide you and the mediator with enough information to equitably resolve the financial issues of your divorce.

Although most mediators will not require that you provide all of this information at the first session, it can be very helpful for the divorcing couple to have a working knowledge about their finances and what is relevant for developing a divorce agreement.

It is also interesting to know that some of the information requested regarding the source, timing, or receipt of certain assets, as well as the reasons for accumulating certain debts, have different legal ramifications depending on the laws in each particular state. As part of the mediation process you will learn either through your mediator or consulting attorney how the laws of your state address these issues.

Why the Forms Help

Forms make you think about what you are doing. They have a way of forcing you to look at what is before embarking on a journey to change things. Clients are often shocked when they look at the actual numbers that document their financial reality. It  is impossible to effectively negotiate for your financial future without knowing your current reality.

It is for this reason that I request that my mediation clients complete forms that document their current expenses (see "What's your Monthly Budget?"). Once the clients clearly understand the expenses, I request that they complete an identical form that sets forth what they expect their expenses to be after the divorce. I also require that they do a similar analysis of their current income and projected income six months after the divorce (see "What's Your Monthly Income?"). The final set of forms describe their current assets and debts (see "What Are Your Assets and Debts?").

During the mediation process clients interact with these forms and constantly make adjustments as they explore their future budgets and opportunities for future financial security.

EVALUATE YOUR MEDIATOR

In addition to some financial preparation, it is important to come to the mediation session with an open mind and to use the first session as an opportunity to assess the mediator. Unless there is an immediate rapport, and both people feel a sense of relief about the process and comfort with the mediator, it is best to continue the search for an appropriate mediator. An investment of one meeting is small considering what is at stake.

As part of this assessment, it is often helpful to ask questions to determine whether this person is best suited for you. Questions about the mediator's years in practice and number of divorce cases are relevant as well as are questions about the handling of specific financial and parenting issues. It is also essential to assess the limitations of your mediator's experience and expertise and their willingness to refer you to attorneys, tax experts, financial planners, appraisers or other appropriate professionals to assist you.

The success of the mediation process is dependent on the competency of the mediator and the compatibility of the mediator's style and personality with that of the couple seeking services. The best way to assess this is to pay attention to the interactions between the mediator and you, the mediator and your spouse, and your spouse and you during that first session. If you pay attention you will instinctively know whether or not to choose a different mediator.

At the End of It

Once you begin work with your mediator, you are on the path to finalizing your divorce. What this means is you have made a commitment to reach an agreement regarding all of the financial and child-related issues of your divorce. With the completion and signing of this agreement comes the freedom to pursue a different life.

In most cases, this means your work is done, and your mediator and attorney will complete all of the other documents required by the court to legalize your divorce. In many jurisdictions, these documents are submitted to the court for the judge's approval, and you do not ever have to enter the courtroom. In other jurisdictions, a short hearing is required. Your mediator or attorney will be able to tell you about your court's requirements.

The agreement that you have reached in mediation will become the court order that specifies the terms of your divorce. Because this court order contains all of the provisions to which you both agreed, enforcement is rarely an issue in mediated divorces.

If you have successfully mediated your divorce "from the inside out," you will have developed certain skills that will help you to evolve into the person you are proud to become.

Good luck to you all!

May your futures be filled with joy
for you and your children.

Appendix:
Financial Data
Collection Package

What's Your Monthly Income?

Notes

MONTHLY INCOME

What's Your Monthly Income (Now)

Spousal support $_____

Child support $_____

Wages $_____

Investment income $_____

Profits from business $_____

Total monthly income $_____

Attach copies of all income tax returns with all W-2s and 1099s. Also attach current profit and loss statement for all businesses.

What's Your Monthly Income (Six Months After the Divorce)

Spousal support $_____

Child support $_____

Wages $_____

Investment income $_____

Profits from business $_____

Total monthly income $_____

What's Your Monthly Budget (Now)

Notes

HOUSING

Rent $\underline{\hspace{2cm}}$
Mortgage (1st) $\underline{\hspace{2cm}}$
Mortgage (2nd) $\underline{\hspace{2cm}}$
Real estate taxes $\underline{\hspace{2cm}}$
Homeowner's insurance $\underline{\hspace{2cm}}$
Condo fee $\underline{\hspace{2cm}}$
General maintenance $\underline{\hspace{2cm}}$
$\underline{\hspace{4cm}}$ $\underline{\hspace{2cm}}$

UTILITIES

Heat $\underline{\hspace{2cm}}$
Electric $\underline{\hspace{2cm}}$
Telephone $\underline{\hspace{2cm}}$
Internet & cable $\underline{\hspace{2cm}}$
Water & sewer $\underline{\hspace{2cm}}$
Trash $\underline{\hspace{2cm}}$
$\underline{\hspace{4cm}}$ $\underline{\hspace{2cm}}$

VEHICLE

Payment $\underline{\hspace{2cm}}$
Insurance $\underline{\hspace{2cm}}$
Gas & oil $\underline{\hspace{2cm}}$
Maintenance $\underline{\hspace{2cm}}$
$\underline{\hspace{3cm}}$ $\underline{\hspace{2cm}}$

INSURANCE (OTHER THAN HOMEOWNER'S AND VEHICLE)

Life $\underline{\hspace{2cm}}$
Health $\underline{\hspace{2cm}}$
Dental $\underline{\hspace{2cm}}$
Disability $\underline{\hspace{2cm}}$
$\underline{\hspace{2cm}}$ $\underline{\hspace{2cm}}$

UNINSURED HEALTH CARE

Medical $\underline{\hspace{2cm}}$
Dental $\underline{\hspace{2cm}}$
Orthodontics $\underline{\hspace{2cm}}$
Medication $\underline{\hspace{2cm}}$
Counseling $\underline{\hspace{2cm}}$
$\underline{\hspace{2cm}}$ $\underline{\hspace{2cm}}$

Notes

LOANS

    Credit cards $_____

    Student loans $_____

    _____ $_____

SAVINGS

    Retirement accounts $_____

    Investments $_____

    Savings $_____

    _____ $_____

GENERAL

    Groceries $_____

    Restaurants $_____

    Entertainment $_____

    Vacations $_____

    Clothing $_____

    Hair care $_____

    Books & magazines $_____

    Education $_____

    Pets $_____

    Gifts $_____

    _____ $_____

CHILDREN

    Clothes $_____

    Daycare $_____

    School supplies $_____

    Activities $_____

    Sports $_____

    Computer $_____

    Camp $_____

    Private school $_____

    School lunches $_____

    College $_____

                          $_____

    _____ $_____

    _____ $_____

    _____ $_____

         Total monthly expenses $_____

What's Your Monthly Budget (Six Months After the Divorce)

Notes

SPOUSAL SUPPORT OBLIGATION $_____

HOUSING
    Rent $_____
    Mortgage (1st) $_____
    Mortgage (2nd) $_____
    Real estate taxes $_____
    Homeowner's insurance $_____
    Condo fee $_____
    General maintenance $_____
    _____ $_____

UTILITIES
    Heat $_____
    Electric $_____
    Telephone $_____
    Internet & cable $_____
    Water & sewer $_____
    Trash $_____
    _____ $_____

VEHICLE
    Payment $_____
    Insurance $_____
    Gas & oil $_____
    Maintenance $_____
    _____ $_____

INSURANCE (OTHER THAN HOMEOWNER'S & VEHICLE)
    Life $_____
    Health $_____
    Dental $_____
    Disability $_____
    _____ $_____

UNINSURED HEALTH CARE
    Medical $_____
    Dental $_____
    Orthodontics $_____
    Medication $_____
    Counseling $_____
    _____ $_____

Notes

LOANS

    Credit cards $_____

    Student loans $_____

    _____ $_____

SAVINGS

    Retirement accounts $_____

    Investments $_____

    Savings $_____

    _____ $_____

GENERAL

    Groceries $_____

    Restaurants $_____

    Entertainment $_____

    Vacations $_____

    Clothing $_____

    Hair care $_____

    Books & magazines $_____

    Education $_____

    Pets $_____

    Gifts $_____

    _____ $_____

CHILDREN

    Clothes $_____

    Daycare $_____

    School supplies $_____

    Activities $_____

    Sports $_____

    Computer $_____

    Camp $_____

    Private school $_____

    School lunches $_____

    College $_____

    Child support $_____

    _____ $_____

    _____ $_____

          Total monthly expenses $_____

What Are Your Assets
and Liabilities

Notes

REAL ESTATE

MARITAL HOME
    Address _____
    Names on deed _____
    Date of purchase _____
    Purchase price _____
        Cash down $ _____
        Original mortgage amount $ _____
    Appraised value as of (date) _____ $ _____
    Market analysis as of (date) _____ $ _____

    1st mortgage balance   Monthly payment
    $ _____ ; $ _____
    2nd mortgage balance   Monthly payment
    $ _____ ; $ _____
                  Equity = $ _____

OTHER REAL ESTATE
    Address _____
    Names on deed _____
    Date of purchase _____
    Purchase price _____
        Cash down $ _____
        Original mortgage amount $ _____
    Appraised value as of (date) _____ $ _____
    Market analysis as of (date) _____ $ _____

    1st mortgage balance   Monthly payment
    $ _____ ; $ _____
    2nd mortgage balance   Monthly payment
    $ _____ ; $ _____
                Equity = $ _____

Attach copies of appraisal or market analysis for all real estate.

Notes

_____

_____

_____

_____

_____

_____

_____

_____

_____

_____

_____

_____

_____

_____

_____

_____

_____

_____

_____

_____

_____

_____

_____

_____

RETIREMENT ACCOUNTS

IRAS

   Financial institution & account # _____

   Type of IRA _____

   Date opened _____

   Current value $ _____

Financial institution & account # _____

   Type of IRA _____

   Date opened _____

   Current value $ _____

401(K)s

   Financial institution and account # _____

   Employer _____

   Date opened _____

   Current value $ _____

   Outstanding loan amount $ _____

Financial institution and account # _____

   Employer _____

   Date opened _____

   Current value $ _____

   Outstanding loan amount $ _____

PENSIONS

   Employer _____

   Date employement commenced _____

   Date employment ended _____

   Salary last year of employment _____

   Vested?   Yes _____   No _____

OTHER RETIREMENT ACCOUNTS _____

Attach a recent statement for each retirement account.

Notes

VEHICLES

TYPE OF VEHICLE

Make, year, and model _____

Lease? Yes _____ No _____

Names on title or lease _____

Monthly payment _____

Balance on outstanding loan _____

Months remaining on lease _____

Estimated fair market value _____

Estimate based on _____

TYPE OF VEHICLE

Make, year, and model _____

Lease? Yes _____ No _____

Names on title or lease _____

Monthly payment _____

Balance on outstanding loan _____

Months remaining on lease _____

Months remaining on lease documents _____

Estimated fair market value _____

Estimate based on _____

Notes

VEHICLES

TYPE OF VEHICLE

Make, year, and model _____

Lease? Yes _____ No _____

Names on title or lease _____

Monthly payment _____

Balance on outstanding loan _____

Months remaining on lease _____

Estimated fair market value _____

Estimate based on _____

TYPE OF VEHICLE

Make, year, and model _____

Lease? Yes _____ No _____

Names on title or lease _____

Monthly payment _____

Balance on outstanding loan _____

Months remaining on lease _____

Estimated fair market value $_____

Estimate based on _____

Notes

INVESTMENT ACCOUNTS (NON-RETIREMENT)

Type of account _____

    Financial institution and account # _____

    Name(s) on account _____

    Current value $ _____

Type of account _____

    Financial institution and account # _____

    Name(s) on account _____

    Current value $ _____

Type of account _____

    Financial institution and account # _____

    Name(s) on account _____

    Current value $ _____

Type of account _____

    Financial institution and account # _____

    Name(s) on account _____

    Current value $ _____

Type of account _____

    Financial institution and account # _____

    Name(s) on account _____

    Current value $ _____

Attach a recent statement for each investment account.

Notes

Inheritances & Gifts (from 3rd Parties)

Description of item _____

_____

_____

    Grantor(s) _____

    Grantee(s) _____

    Date received _____

    Estimated fair market value $ _____

    Basis for estimate _____

Description of item _____

_____

_____

    Grantor(s) _____

    Grantee(s) _____

    Date received _____

    Estimated fair market value $ _____

    Basis for estimate _____

Description of item _____

_____

_____

    Grantor(s) _____

    Grantee(s) _____

    Date received _____

    Estimated fair market value $ _____

    Basis for estimate _____

Notes

TANGIBLE PERSONAL PROPERTY OF VALUE
Valued at more than $5,000

Description of item _____

_____

    Date received _____

    Source of funds to purchase _____

    Estimated fair market value $ _____

    Basis for estimate _____

Description of item _____

_____

    Date received _____

    Source of funds to purchase _____

    Estimated fair market value $ _____

    Basis for estimate _____

Description of item _____

_____

    Date received _____

    Source of funds to purchase _____

    Estimated fair market value $ _____

    Basis for estimate _____

Description of item _____

_____

    Date received _____

    Source of funds to purchase _____

    Estimated fair market value $ _____

    Basis for estimate _____

Notes

BUSINESS INTERESTS

Name of business _____

    Type of entity _____

    Date of formation _____

    List all owners, shareholders, or members with approximate % of equity for each _____

    _____

    _____

    Description of products or services provided _____

    _____

Gross sales year to date

    $ _____

Gross sales for last 3 years

    $ _____

    $ _____

    $ _____

Value of business assets

    $ _____

Outstanding debt

    $ _____

Attach copies of the 3 most recent tax returns, a current profit and loss statement, and a current balance sheet for each business.

Notes

PERSONAL DEBT

Name of creditor & account # ———————————————
    Outstanding balance $ ——————————————
    Monthly payment $ ————————————————
    Interest rate ————————————————————
    Name(s) of debtors on the account ——————————
    Account current?   Yes ———— No ————
    Purpose of the loan ————————————————

Name of creditor & account # ———————————————
    Outstanding balance $————————————————
    Monthly payment $ ————————————————
    Interest rate ————————————————————
    Name(s) of debtors on the account ——————————
    Account current?   Yes ———— No ————
    Purpose of the loan ————————————————

Name of creditor & account # ———————————————
    Outstanding balance $ ——————————————
    Monthly payment $————————————————
    Interest rate ————————————————————
    Name(s) of debtors on the account ——————————
    Account current?   Yes ———— No ————
    Purpose of the loan ————————————————

Name of creditor & account # ———————————————
    Outstanding balance $ ——————————————
    Monthly payment $————————————————
    Interest rate ————————————————————
    Name(s) of debtors on the account ——————————
    Account current?   Yes ———— No ————
    Purpose of the loan ————————————————

Notes

PERSONAL DEBT

Name of creditor & account # _____

    Outstanding balance $ _____

    Monthly payment $ _____

    Interest rate _____

    Name(s) of debtors on the account _____

    Account current?   Yes _____ No _____

    Purpose of the loan _____

Name of creditor & account # _____

    Outstanding balance $ _____

    Monthly payment $ _____

    Interest rate _____

    Name(s) of debtors on the account _____

    Account current?   Yes _____ No _____

    Purpose of the loan _____

Name of creditor & account # _____

    Outstanding balance $ _____

    Monthly payment $ _____

    Interest rate _____

    Name(s) of debtors on the account _____

    Account current?   Yes _____ No _____

    Purpose of the loan _____

Attach copies of recent statements for each account.

About the Author

Ora Schwartzberg (formerly Carol Ann Borofsky) has been practicing law since 1985 and has also been a mediation practitioner for fifteen years. She is a graduate of Vermont Law School. Prior to that she received a master's degree in counseling from SUNY, Platts-burgh (New York), and an undergraduate degree in education from Temple University in Philadelphia. She has had careers as an inner-city high school teacher (English) and as a counselor prior to attending law school. Attor-ney Schwartzberg practiced law in Saranac Lake and Lake Placid, New York, until 2001 when she passed the New Hampshire Bar and relocated to Bedford, New Hampshire.

Although a large part of her practice involves divorce mediation, Attorney Schwartzberg also mediates cases involving small business, real estate, and family issues unrelated to divorce. She is an active member of the New Hampshire Bar Association, presently serving as a member of the Legislative Committee and cochair of the Alternative Dispute Resolution Section. She is also a New Hampshire-certified marital mediator and serves as a mediator for the New Hampshire Superior Courts. She now maintains offices in Concord and Piermont, New Hampshire. Visit her website at www.nhlawyer.net.

Notes

Notes

Notes

CPSIA information can be obtained at www.ICGtesting.com
Printed in the USA
LVOW040534220312

274272LV00001B/231/P